1 Base, 50 pizzas

Rachel Carter

First published in 2011

LOVE FOOD is an imprint of Parragon Books Ltd

Parragon
Queen Street House
4 Queen Street
Bath BA1 1HE, UK

ISBN: 978-1-4454-3951-8

Printed in China

Written by Rachel Carter
Photography by Mike Cooper
Home economy by Lincoln Jefferson

Notes for the Reader
This book uses both metric and imperial measurements. Follow
the same units of measurement throughout; do not mix metric and
imperial. All spoon measurements are level: teaspoons are assumed
to be 5 ml, and tablespoons are assumed to be 15 ml. Unless
otherwise stated, milk is assumed to be full fat, eggs and individual
vegetables are medium, and pepper is freshly ground black pepper.

The times given are an approximate guide only. Preparation times
differ according to the techniques used by different people and the
cooking times may also vary from those given. Optional ingredients,
variations or serving suggestions have not been included in the
calculations.

Recipes using raw or very lightly cooked eggs should be avoided
by infants, the elderly, pregnant women, convalescents and anyone
suffering from an illness. Pregnant and breastfeeding women are
advised to avoid eating peanuts and peanut products. Sufferers
from nut allergies should be aware that some of the ready-made
ingredients used in the recipes in this book may contain nuts. Always
check the packaging before use.

Contents

Introduction

The origins of pizza are not clear cut; it seems that the idea was originally taken not from the Italians but from the Greeks who ate pieces of circular flat bread flavoured with oil, spices and herbs. It wasn't until these breads found their way into the streets of Naples in the 18th century that they became known as pizzas. Their popularity rose when in the mid-1800s the Italian queen, Margherita, and her husband were travelling around Italy and discovered their love of this popular street food. They were inspired to ask their chefs to work on different flavour combinations using bread as the base and the ubiquitous margherita pizza was invented using the colours of the Italian flag with tomatoes, mozzarella and fresh basil as the topping.

Of course pizzas are now a world-wide phenomenon and the choice of toppings is endless. This book features five chapters, starting with vegetable, then meat-based pizzas, fish and seafood, nice and spicy and finally a novelty chapter full of fun and unique ideas!

A basic recipe for the dough on page 8 forms the basis of all the recipes. Sometimes the dough will have additions of herbs or spices and it may be rolled out into different sizes and shapes, but essentially it is the same recipe throughout. The basic dough recipe makes enough for two good-sized pizzas based on a thin crust pizza, which will make one large thicker crust version.

The Dough

When making pizza dough, the best and most authentic dough is a bread-based one, using yeast as the raising agent. The recipes in this book use easy-blend dried yeast (also known as fast-acting yeast), which is available in sachets or tubs. If you prefer to use fresh yeast then this is available to buy in good bakeries. You would need to use 10 g/¼ oz of fresh yeast per 300 g/10½ oz flour (or approximately double the amount of fresh to dried yeast) with 1 teaspoon of sugar mixed with the warm water and allowed to stand in a warm place for 20 minutes until frothy. If using easy-blend yeast there is no need for this step. Once the fresh yeast mixture is frothy, the recipe can then be followed in the normal way.

The flour that you use is also key to a good dough. Strong plain flour is the best since it has a high gluten content which gives a good rise during baking, or you could substitute wholemeal, granary or spelt flour for the plain flour, or use gluten-free versions.

The most common way of making bread dough is to allow it to prove in a warm place for an hour or so to double in size. However, the yeast will still be effective if the dough is left in a cold place or refrigerator overnight. Any leftover dough can also be frozen and will still rise and cook normally when defrosted. Just wrap the dough tightly in clingfilm and keep frozen for up to six months.

Kneading

Kneading is the process which develops the gluten in the dough and allows it to rise during proving to give a light-textured bread. This vigorous method of stretching will typically take about 10 minutes by hand or around 3–5 minutes with an electric mixer and dough hook. You will know when the dough is ready as it will become smooth and very elastic.

A good check to test whether your dough is kneaded fully is to take a small piece of dough and do 'the window test'. Stretch the dough and if it is elastic and pulls apart without tearing then it is ready. If it tears, continue kneading for a few more minutes.

Top Tips

If the dough becomes too wet during mixing then just knead a little more flour into it. If it's very stretchy and difficult to roll out then leave it for 10 minutes before trying again.

When rolling out the dough use a rolling pin and keep turning it a quarter turn before rolling again until it reaches the required size. You'll find that you need far more pressure than when rolling pastry dough.

If you have a pizza stone then these are great for ensuring that the base is fully cooked. Just preheat it first. If you don't have one, use a preheated baking tray. A pizza peel is a flat wooden paddle used for getting pizzas on and off hot pizza stones. They can be useful but are by no means essential.

The basic dough recipe can also be used to make delicious garlic bread. Simply shape into a thick round after proving and drizzle with a little extra virgin olive oil and some rock salt and a little fresh chopped rosemary. Bake for 20-25 minutes and then brush with garlic butter.

If you want to get ahead, or when making pizzas in bulk, simply make the dough in advance, allow to prove, then roll out, place on baking trays and cover with baking paper until you are ready to use.

Pizza Sauce Recipe

The recipes in this book use ready-made sauces as the base of the pizza. If you wish to make your own here is a quick recipe:

1 tbsp olive oil

1 garlic clove, crushed

1 onion, finely chopped

400 g/14 oz canned chopped tomatoes

1 tbsp tomato purée

1 tsp dried oregano

salt and pepper

Heat the oil in a saucepan, add the garlic and onion and sauté for 5-6 minutes, or until softened. Add the remaining ingredients and season to taste with salt and pepper. Simmer for about 10 minutes, or until the mixture is reduced slightly and suitable for spreading.

Home-made pizza sauce can be stored in a screw-top jar in the refrigerator for up to a week.

You could also use passata, or even tomato purée, although this has a very intense flavour and is probably better diluted with a little water first. Peeled and finely diced fresh tomatoes may also be used, creating a different texture. Of course, not all pizzas include tomatoes or tomato sauce. A great and tasty alternative is using pesto.

Basic Pizza Dough

Makes two x 26-cm/10½-inch round pizzas; or
four x 19-cm/7½-inch round pizzas; or
one x 38 x 26-cm/15 x 10½-inch rectangular pizza

300 g/10½ oz strong white flour, plus extra for dusting
1 tsp easy-blend dried yeast
1½ tsp salt
175 ml/6 fl oz hand-hot water
1 tbsp olive oil, plus extra for kneading

1. Sift the flour into a mixing bowl and add the yeast and salt, making a small well in the top. Mix the water and oil together and pour into the bowl, using a round-bladed knife to gradually combine all the flour to make a sticky dough.

2. Lightly flour the work surface and your hands and knead the dough for about 10 minutes, until it is smooth and elastic.

3. Cover the dough with some lightly oiled clingfilm or a damp tea towel and leave to rise for about an hour, or until it has doubled in size.

This is the basic recipe on which all 50 variations of pizza in the book are based.

For each recipe the basic mix is highlighted (*) for easy reference, so all you have to do is follow the steps each time and you'll never run out of ideas for tempting tasty pizza!

Please note that the basic ingredients may vary from time to time, so please check these carefully.

Vegetable Delights

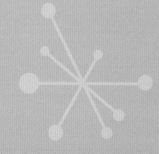

Margherita Pizza

1. Make the pizza dough as described on page 8. Knock back the dough by gently kneading for about a minute, then divide into two balls. To roll out the dough, flatten each ball, then, using a rolling pin, roll out on a lightly floured work surface, giving a quarter turn between each roll.

2. Preheat the oven to 220°C/425°F/Gas Mark 7. Place the pizza bases on two baking trays, using a rolling pin to transfer them from the work surface.

3. Divide the pizza sauce between the two pizza bases, spreading almost to the edges. Scatter over the garlic and then top with the mozzarella cheese and Parmesan cheese. Season to taste with salt and pepper and drizzle over the olive oil.

4. Bake in the preheated oven for 10–12 minutes, or until the cheese is melting and turning golden and the bases are crisp underneath. Garnish with basil leaves and serve immediately.

Makes 2 pizzas

* 1 quantity Basic Pizza Dough

Topping
200 g/7 oz ready-prepared tomato pizza sauce

2 garlic cloves, crushed

250 g/9 oz mozzarella cheese in brine, drained and roughly torn

25 g/1 oz Parmesan cheese shavings

2 tbsp extra virgin olive oil

salt and pepper

fresh basil leaves, to garnish

Four Cheese Pizza

1. Make the pizza dough as described on page 8. Knock back the dough by gently kneading for about a minute, then divide into two balls. To roll out the dough, flatten each ball, then, using a rolling pin, roll out on a lightly floured work surface, giving a quarter turn between each roll.

2. Preheat the oven to 220°C/425°F/Gas Mark 7. Place the pizza bases on two baking trays, using a rolling pin to transfer them from the work surface.

3. Spread the pizza sauce over the pizza bases, spreading almost to the edges. Arrange the cheese on the bases, with one type of cheese on each quarter.

4. Bake in the preheated oven for 10–12 minutes, or until the cheese is melting and turning golden and the bases are crisp underneath. Season to taste with pepper and serve immediately.

Makes 2 pizzas

* 1 quantity Basic Pizza Dough

Topping
200 g/7 oz ready-prepared tomato pizza sauce

250 g/9 oz mozzarella cheese in brine, drained and roughly torn

100 g/3½ oz blue cheese, crumbled

100 g/3½ oz Cheddar cheese, grated

100 g/3½ oz Brie, thinly sliced

pepper

Fiorentina Pizza

1. Make the pizza dough as described on page 8. Knock back the dough by gently kneading for about a minute, then divide into four balls. To roll out the dough, flatten each ball, then, using a rolling pin, roll out on a lightly floured work surface, giving a quarter turn between each roll.

2. Preheat the oven to 220°C/425°F/Gas Mark 7. Place the pizza bases on two baking trays, using a rolling pin to transfer them from the work surface.

3. Put the spinach into a small saucepan, place over a low heat and cook for 1–2 minutes, or until it has wilted. Drain the spinach through a sieve and press down with the back of a spoon to remove any excess water.

4. Divide the pizza sauce between the four pizza bases, spreading almost to the edges. Scatter over the garlic, top with the spinach and olives and drizzle over the garlic oil.

5. Bake in the preheated oven for 8–10 minutes, then remove from the oven and make a small indentation in the centre of each pizza. Pour an egg into each indentation, scatter over the cheese and season to taste with salt and pepper. Return to the oven and bake for a further 3–5 minutes, or until the eggs are just cooked and the bases are crisp underneath. Serve immediately.

Makes 4 small pizzas

1 quantity Basic Pizza Dough

Topping

250 g/9 oz spinach, washed and drained

200 g/7 oz ready-prepared tomato pizza sauce

2 garlic cloves, finely chopped

25 g/1 oz black olives, stoned and halved

2 tbsp garlic olive oil

4 eggs

85 g/3 oz finely grated Grana Padano cheese or Parmesan cheese

salt and pepper

Vegetable Four Seasons Pizza

1. Make the pizza dough as described on page 8. Knock back the dough by gently kneading for about a minute. Roll out the dough on a lightly floured work surface to a 38 x 26-cm/ 15 x 10½-inch rectangle.

2. Preheat the oven to 220°C/425°F/Gas Mark 7. Place the pizza base on a 38 x 26-cm/15 x 10½-inch baking tray, using a rolling pin to transfer it from the work surface.

3. Spread the pizza sauce over the pizza base, almost to the edges. Place the onion and red pepper pieces on one quarter of the base, the olives and capers on the next quarter, the mushrooms on the next and the green pepper and artichoke pieces on the fourth quarter. Scatter over the cheese and season to taste with pepper.

4. Bake in the preheated oven for 15–20 minutes, or until the cheese is melting and turning golden and the base is crisp underneath. Serve immediately.

Makes 1 large pizza

1 quantity Basic Pizza Dough

Topping

200 g/7 oz ready-prepared tomato pizza sauce

½ red onion, finely sliced

½ red pepper, deseeded and finely sliced

25 g/1 oz black olives, stoned and halved

1 tbsp capers in brine, drained

85 g/3 oz button mushrooms, sliced

½ green pepper, deseeded and finely sliced

50 g/1¾ oz artichoke hearts in oil, drained and halved

250 g/9 oz mozzarella cheese in brine, drained and roughly torn

pepper

Garlic Mushroom & Gruyère Pizza

1. Make the pizza dough as described on page 8. Knock back the dough by gently kneading for about a minute, then divide into two balls. To roll out the dough, flatten each ball, then, using a rolling pin, roll out on a lightly floured work surface, giving a quarter turn between each roll.

2. Preheat the oven to 220°C/425°F/Gas Mark 7. Place the pizza bases on two baking trays, using a rolling pin to transfer them from the work surface.

3. Divide the pizza sauce between the two pizza bases, spreading almost to the edges.

4. Heat the oil in a frying pan over a medium heat, then add the garlic and mushrooms and sauté gently over a medium heat for 4–5 minutes, until softened. Drain on kitchen paper and then scatter over the pizza bases. Top with the cheese and season to taste with salt and pepper.

5. Bake in the preheated oven for 10–12 minutes, or until the cheese is melting and turning golden and the bases are crisp underneath. Garnish with the chopped parsley and serve immediately.

Makes 2 pizzas

* 1 quantity Basic Pizza Dough

Topping
200 g/7 oz ready-prepared tomato pizza sauce

1 tbsp olive oil

2 garlic cloves, crushed

175 g/6 oz large field mushrooms, wiped and thinly sliced

175 g/6 oz Gruyère cheese, grated

salt and pepper

chopped fresh flat-leaf parsley, to garnish

Spicy Mozzarella Pizza

① Make the pizza dough as described on page 8. Knock back the dough by gently kneading for about a minute, then divide into two balls. To roll out the dough, flatten each ball, then, using a rolling pin, roll out on a lightly floured work surface, giving a quarter turn between each roll.

② Preheat the oven to 220°C/425°F/Gas Mark 7. Place the pizza bases on two baking trays, using a rolling pin to transfer them from the work surface.

③ Divide the pizza sauce between the two pizza bases, spreading almost to the edges. Scatter over the onion, olives, cheese and chilli flakes. Drizzle over the oil and season to taste with salt and pepper.

④ Bake in the preheated oven for 10–12 minutes, or until the cheese is melting and turning golden and the bases are crisp underneath. Serve immediately.

Makes 2 pizzas

✳ 1 quantity Basic Pizza Dough

Topping
200 g/7 oz ready-prepared tomato pizza sauce

1 small red onion, finely sliced

25 g/1 oz mixed olives, stoned and halved

250 g/9 oz buffalo mozzarella cheese in brine, drained and roughly torn

½ tsp dried chilli flakes

2 tsp extra virgin olive oil

salt and pepper

Vegetable Heaven Pizza

1. Make the pizza dough as described on page 8. Knock back the dough by gently kneading for about a minute, then divide into two balls. To roll out the dough, flatten each ball, then, using a rolling pin, roll out on a lightly floured work surface, giving a quarter turn between each roll.

2. Preheat the oven to 220°C/425°F/Gas Mark 7. Place the pizza bases on two baking trays, using a rolling pin to transfer them from the work surface.

3. Bring a small saucepan of lightly salted water to the boil. Add the asparagus spears and cook for 2–3 minutes. Drain and plunge into ice cold water for 1–2 minutes (to retain the bright green colour). Drain well.

4. Divide the pizza sauce between the two pizza bases, spreading almost to the edges. Place the cooked asparagus all around the pizza bases with the cut ends at the outside edges and the tips in the centre. Scatter over the remaining vegetables, tomatoes and olives and top with the cheese. Season to taste with salt and pepper.

5. Bake in the preheated oven for 12–15 minutes, until the cheese is melting and turning golden and the bases are crisp underneath. Serve immediately.

Makes 2 pizzas

✳ 1 quantity Basic Pizza Dough

Topping

150 g/5½ oz asparagus spears, trimmed

200 g/7 oz ready-prepared tomato pizza sauce

175 g/6 oz artichoke hearts in oil, drained and quartered

200 g/7 oz button mushrooms, wiped and thinly sliced

125 g/4½ oz cherry tomatoes, thinly sliced

50 g/1¾ oz mixed olives, stoned and halved

250 g/9 oz mozzarella cheese in brine, drained and roughly torn

salt and pepper

Roasted Red Pepper & Asparagus Pizza

1. Make the pizza dough as described on page 8. Knock back the dough by gently kneading for about a minute, then divide into two balls. To roll out the dough, flatten each ball, then, using a rolling pin, roll out on a lightly floured work surface, giving a quarter turn between each roll.

2. Preheat the oven to 220°C/425°F/Gas Mark 7. Place the pizza bases on two baking trays, using a rolling pin to transfer them from the work surface.

3. Bring a small saucepan of lightly salted water to the boil. Add the asparagus spears and cook for 2–3 minutes. Drain and plunge into ice cold water for 1–2 minutes (to retain the bright green colour). Drain well.

4. Divide the pizza sauce between the two pizza bases, spreading almost to the edges. Scatter over the cooked asparagus, red pepper and cheese. Season to taste with salt and pepper.

5. Bake in the preheated oven for 10–12 minutes, or until the cheese is melting and turning golden and the bases are crisp underneath. Serve immediately.

Makes 2 pizzas

* 1 quantity Basic Pizza Dough

Topping
150 g/5½ oz asparagus spears, trimmed

200 g/7 oz ready-prepared tomato pizza sauce

1 roasted red pepper in brine, drained and thinly sliced

250 g/9 oz mozzarella cheese in brine, drained and roughly torn

salt and pepper

Goat's Cheese & Olive Pizza

1. Make the pizza dough as described on page 8. Knock back the dough by gently kneading for about a minute, then divide into two balls. To roll out the dough, flatten each ball, then, using a rolling pin, roll out on a lightly floured work surface, giving a quarter turn between each roll.

2. Preheat the oven to 220°C/425°F/Gas Mark 7. Place the pizza bases on two baking trays, using a rolling pin to transfer them from the work surface.

3. Divide the pizza sauce between the two pizza bases, spreading almost to the edges. Scatter over the tomatoes, olives and cheese. Sprinkle over the herbs and season to taste with salt and pepper.

4. Bake in the preheated oven for 10–12 minutes, or until the cheese is melting and turning golden and the bases are crisp underneath. Serve immediately.

Makes 2 pizzas

1 quantity Basic Pizza Dough

Topping

200 g/7 oz ready-prepared tomato pizza sauce

8 cherry tomatoes, thinly sliced

50 g/1¾ oz black or green olives, stoned and thinly sliced

200 g/7 oz soft goat's cheese, thinly sliced

2 tsp herbes de Provence

salt and pepper

Sun-dried Tomato & Ricotta Cheese Calzone

1. Make the pizza dough as described on page 8. Knock back the dough by gently kneading for about a minute, then divide into two balls. To roll out the dough, flatten each ball, then, using a rolling pin, roll out on a lightly floured work surface, giving a quarter turn between each roll.

2. Preheat the oven to 220°C/425°F/Gas Mark 7. Place the pizza bases on two baking trays, using a rolling pin to transfer them from the work surface.

3. Divide the pizza sauce between the two pizza bases, spreading almost to the edges. Scatter the tomatoes over one half of each base, then spoon the cheese evenly over the tomatoes. Sprinkle over the herbs and season to taste with salt and pepper.

4. Brush the edges of the bases with a little water, then fold them over the filling to make two half-moon-shaped calzones. Seal the edges all the way around by folding a little of the dough over and pinching the edges together. Make small holes in the top of each calzone with the tip of a knife.

5. Bake in the preheated oven for 10–12 minutes, or until the tops are golden and the bases are crisp underneath. Serve immediately.

Makes 2 calzones

✳ 1 quantity Basic Pizza Dough

Filling

200 g/7 oz ready-prepared tomato pizza sauce

200 g/7 oz sun-dried tomatoes in oil, drained and halved

150 g/5½ oz ricotta cheese

1 tsp dried mixed herbs

salt and pepper

Meat Lovers

Meat Feast Pizza

1. Make the pizza dough as described on page 8. Knock back the dough by gently kneading for about a minute, then divide into two balls. To roll out the dough, flatten each ball, then, using a rolling pin, roll out on a lightly floured work surface, giving a quarter turn between each roll.

2. Preheat the oven to 220°C/425°F/Gas Mark 7. Place the pizza bases on two baking trays, using a rolling pin to transfer them from the work surface.

3. Divide the pizza sauce between the two pizza bases, spreading almost to the edges. Scatter over the pastrami, ham and pepperoni, top with the mushrooms and red pepper and finish with the cheese and herbs.

4. Bake in the preheated oven for 10–15 minutes, or until the cheese is melting and turning golden and the bases are crisp underneath. Serve immediately.

Makes 2 pizzas

* 1 quantity Basic Pizza Dough

Topping
200 g/7 oz ready-prepared tomato pizza sauce

90 g/3¼ oz pastrami, roughly chopped

100 g/3½ oz cooked, sliced ham, roughly chopped

100 g/3½ oz pepperoni, thinly sliced

100 g/3½ oz mushrooms, thinly sliced

½ red pepper, deseeded and thinly sliced

200 g/7 oz Cheddar cheese, grated

¼ tsp dried herbes de Provence

Piccante Pizza

1. Make the pizza dough as described on page 8. Knock back the dough by gently kneading for about a minute. Using a rolling pin, roll out the dough on a lightly floured work surface to a 38 x 26-cm/15 x 10½-inch rectangle.

2. Heat the oil in a medium-size saucepan over a medium heat, then add the onion and garlic and gently sauté for 4–5 minutes, until starting to soften. Add the chillies and red pepper and cook for a further 1–2 minutes, then add the beef mince and continue to sauté over a medium–high heat for 4–5 minutes, until lightly browned all over.

3. Add the tomato purée and cook for 1 minute, stirring all the time. Stir in the water and season to taste with salt and pepper, then cover and simmer for 10–15 minutes, stirring occasionally, until the meat is thoroughly cooked. Remove from the heat and leave to cool.

4. Preheat the oven to 230°C/450°F/Gas Mark 8. Place the pizza base on a 38 x 26-cm/15 x 10½-inch rectangular baking tray, using a rolling pin to transfer it from the work surface. Spread the pizza sauce over the pizza base then top with the beef mixture and scatter over the cheeses.

5. Bake in the preheated oven for 15–20 minutes, or until the cheese is melting and turning golden and the base is crisp underneath. Serve immediately.

Makes 1 large pizza

❋ 1 quantity Basic Pizza Dough

Topping

1 tbsp vegetable oil

1 onion, finely chopped

2 garlic cloves, crushed

2 red chillies, deseeded and finely chopped

1 red pepper, deseeded and chopped

500 g/1lb 2 oz lean beef mince

2 tbsp tomato purée

200 ml/7 fl oz cold water

200 g/7 oz ready-prepared tomato pizza sauce

100 g/3½ oz Cheddar cheese, grated

125 g/4½ oz mozzarella cheese in brine, drained and roughly torn

salt and pepper

American Hot Pizza

1. Make the pizza dough as described on page 8. Knock back the dough by gently kneading for about a minute, then divide into two balls. To roll out the dough, flatten each ball, then, using a rolling pin, roll out on a lightly floured work surface, giving a quarter turn between each roll.

2. Preheat the oven to 220°C/425°F/Gas Mark 7. Place the pizza bases on two baking trays, using a rolling pin to transfer them from the work surface.

3. Divide the pizza sauce between the two pizza bases, spreading almost to the edges. Scatter over the onion, pepperoni, jalapeño peppers and yellow pepper. Top with the cheese and season to taste with pepper.

4. Bake in the preheated oven for 10–12 minutes, or until the cheese is melting and turning golden and the bases are crisp underneath. Serve immediately.

Makes 2 pizzas

✳ 1 quantity Basic Pizza Dough

Topping
200 g/7 oz ready-prepared tomato pizza sauce

1 small red onion, finely sliced

250 g/9 oz hot pepperoni, thinly sliced

50 g/1¾ oz sweet, hot red jalapeño peppers in oil, drained and sliced

1 yellow pepper, deseeded and finely sliced

150 g/5½ oz Cheddar cheese, grated

pepper

14

Siciliana Pizza

1. Make the pizza dough as described on page 8. Knock back the dough by gently kneading for about a minute. Using a rolling pin, roll out the dough to a 38 x 26-cm/ 15 x 10½-inch rectangle on a lightly floured work surface.

2. Preheat the oven to 230°C/450°F/Gas Mark 8. Place the pizza base on a 38 x 26-cm/15 x 10½-inch rectangular baking tray, using a rolling pin to transfer it from the work surface.

3. Spread the pizza sauce on the pizza base, spreading almost to the edges. Scatter over the garlic, ham, olives, artichoke hearts and tomatoes. Drizzle over the reserved oil and top with the mozzarella cheese and Parmesan cheese. Season to taste with pepper.

4. Bake in the preheated oven for 12–15 minutes, or until the cheese is melting and turning golden and the base is crisp underneath. Serve immediately.

Makes 1 large pizza

✳ 1 quantity Basic Pizza Dough

Topping
200 g/7 oz ready-prepared tomato pizza sauce

1 garlic clove, finely chopped

175 g/6 oz cooked ham, torn into strips

50 g/1¾ oz mixed olives, stoned and halved

200 g/7 oz artichoke hearts in oil, drained and cut into quarters

200 g/7 oz sun-dried tomatoes in oil, drained and halved, reserving 1 tbsp oil

150 g/5½ oz mozzarella cheese in brine, drained and roughly torn

100 g/3½ oz Parmesan cheese shavings

pepper

15

La Reine Pizza

1. Make the pizza dough as described on page 8. Knock back the dough by gently kneading for about a minute, then divide into two balls. To roll out the dough, flatten each ball, then, using a rolling pin, roll out on a lightly floured work surface, giving a quarter turn between each roll.

2. Preheat the oven to 220°C/425°F/Gas Mark 7. Place the pizza bases on two baking trays, using a rolling pin to transfer them from the work surface.

3. Divide the pizza sauce between the two pizza bases, spreading almost to the edges. Scatter over the ham, olives and mushrooms and top with the cheese. Season to taste with salt and pepper.

4. Bake in the preheated oven for 10–12 minutes, or until the cheese is melting and turning golden and the bases are crisp underneath. Serve immediately.

Makes 2 pizzas

* 1 quantity Basic Pizza Dough

Topping

200 g/7 oz ready-prepared tomato pizza sauce

175 g/6 oz sliced, cooked ham, torn into strips

50 g/1¾ oz mixed olives, stoned and halved

100 g/3½ oz button mushrooms, thinly sliced

250 g/9 oz mozzarella cheese in brine, drained and roughly torn

salt and pepper

16

Hawaiian Pizza

1. Make the pizza dough as described on page 8. Knock back the dough by gently kneading for about a minute, then divide into two balls. To roll out the dough, flatten each ball, then, using a rolling pin, roll out on a lightly floured work surface, giving a quarter turn between each roll.

2. Preheat the oven to 220°C/425°F/Gas Mark 7. Place the pizza bases on two baking trays, using a rolling pin to transfer them from the work surface.

3. Divide the pizza sauce between the two pizza bases, spreading almost to the edges. Scatter over the ham and pineapple and top with the mozzarella cheese and Cheddar cheese.

4. Bake in the preheated oven for 10–12 minutes, or until the cheese is melting and turning golden and the bases are crisp underneath. Serve immediately.

Makes 2 pizzas

* 1 quantity Basic Pizza Dough

Topping
200 g/7 oz ready-prepared tomato pizza sauce

200 g/7 oz cooked, sliced ham, roughly chopped

100 g/3½ oz fresh pineapple, peeled, cored and cut into small cubes

125 g/4½ oz mozzarella cheese in brine, drained and roughly torn

100 g/3½ oz Cheddar cheese, grated

Prosciutto & Rocket Pizza

1. Make the pizza dough as described on page 8. Knock back the dough by gently kneading for about a minute, then divide into two balls. To roll out the dough, flatten each ball, then, using a rolling pin, roll out on a lightly floured work surface, giving a quarter turn between each roll.

2. Preheat the oven to 220°C/425°F/Gas Mark 7. Place the pizza bases on two baking trays, using a rolling pin to transfer them from the work surface.

3. Divide the pizza sauce between the two pizza bases, spreading almost to the edges. Scatter over the prosciutto and olives and top with the mozzarella cheese.

4. Bake in the preheated oven for 10–15 minutes, or until the cheese is melting and turning golden and the bases are crisp underneath.

5. Remove from the oven, drizzle over the oil, season to taste with salt and pepper and garnish with the rocket. Serve immediately.

Makes 2 pizzas

1 quantity Basic Pizza Dough

Topping

200 g/7 oz ready-prepared tomato pizza sauce

200 g/7 oz thinly sliced prosciutto, torn into large pieces

50 g/1¾ oz mixed olives, stoned and halved

250 g/9 oz buffalo mozzarella cheese in brine, drained and roughly torn

1 tbsp extra virgin olive oil

salt and pepper

fresh rocket leaves, to garnish

Melted Brie & Bacon Pizza

1. Make the pizza dough as described on page 8. Knock back the dough by gently kneading for about a minute, then divide into two balls. To roll out the dough, flatten each ball, then, using a rolling pin, roll out on a lightly floured work surface, giving a quarter turn between each roll.

2. Preheat the oven to 240°C/475°F/Gas Mark 9. Place the pizza bases on two baking trays, using a rolling pin to transfer them from the work surface.

3. Divide the pizza sauce between the two pizza bases, spreading almost to the edges. Scatter the bacon over the bases and bake in the preheated oven for 6–8 minutes.

4. Remove the pizzas from the oven and lay the cheese over the top. Return to the oven for a further 6–8 minutes, or until the cheese is melting and turning golden and the bases are crisp underneath.

5. Season to taste with salt and pepper, garnish with the rocket leaves and serve immediately.

Makes 2 pizzas

✳ 1 quantity Basic Pizza Dough

Topping
200 g/7 oz ready-prepared tomato pizza sauce
200 g/7 oz smoked streaky bacon, finely chopped
250 g/9 oz Brie, thinly sliced
salt and pepper
fresh rocket leaves, to garnish

Pesto Chicken Pizza

1. Make the pizza dough as described on page 8. Knock back the dough by gently kneading for about a minute, then divide into two balls. To roll out the dough, flatten each ball, then, using a rolling pin, roll out on a lightly floured work surface, giving a quarter turn between each roll.

2. Preheat the oven to 220°C/425°F/Gas Mark 7. Place the pizza bases on two baking trays, using a rolling pin to transfer them from the work surface.

3. Divide the pesto between the two pizza bases, spreading almost to the edges. Scatter over the chicken, sweetcorn and tomatoes. Top with the cheese and season to taste with salt and pepper.

4. Bake in the preheated oven for 10–12 minutes, or until the cheese is melting and turning golden and the bases are crisp underneath. Serve immediately.

Makes 2 pizzas

1 quantity Basic Pizza Dough

Topping
8 tbsp ready-prepared pesto

175 g/6 oz cooked chicken, torn into strips

100 g/3½ oz canned sweetcorn

6 cherry tomatoes, thinly sliced

250 g/9 oz mozzarella cheese in brine, drained and roughly torn

salt and pepper

Chicken & Spinach Pizza

1. Make the pizza dough as described on page 8. Knock back the dough by gently kneading for about a minute, then divide into two balls. To roll out the dough, flatten each ball, then, using a rolling pin, roll out on a lightly floured work surface, giving a quarter turn between each roll.

2. Preheat the oven to 220°C/425°F/Gas Mark 7. Place the pizza bases on two baking trays, using a rolling pin to transfer them from the work surface.

3. Place the spinach in a small saucepan over a medium heat and cook for 1–2 minutes, until it has wilted. Drain through a sieve and press down with the back of a spoon to remove any excess water.

4. Divide the pizza sauce between the two pizza bases, spreading almost to the edges. Scatter the spinach, chicken and red pepper over the pizza bases and top with the cheese. Season to taste with salt and pepper.

5. Bake in the preheated oven for 10–12 minutes, or until the cheese is melting and turning golden and the bases are crisp underneath. Serve immediately.

Makes 2 pizzas

✳ 1 quantity Basic Pizza Dough

Topping
250 g/9 oz spinach, washed and drained

200 g/7 oz ready-prepared tomato pizza sauce

150 g/5½ oz cooked chicken, roughly torn

1 large ready-roasted red pepper, drained and thinly sliced

250 g/9 oz light mozzarella cheese in brine, drained and roughly torn

salt and pepper

Fish & Seafood

21

Tuna, Olive, Sun-dried Tomato & Ricotta Cheese Pizza

1. Make the pizza dough as described on page 8. Knock back the dough by gently kneading for about a minute, then divide into two balls. To roll out the dough, flatten each ball, then, using a rolling pin, roll out on a lightly floured work surface, giving a quarter turn between each roll.

2. Preheat the oven to 220°C/425°F/Gas Mark 7. Place the pizza bases on two baking trays, using a rolling pin to transfer them from the work surface.

3. Divide the pizza sauce between the two pizza bases, spreading almost to the edges. Scatter over the tuna, tomatoes, olives and herbs. Spoon small amounts of the cheese evenly over the bases in small amounts, then drizzle over the reserved oil and season to taste with salt and pepper.

4. Bake in the preheated oven for 10–12 minutes, or until the cheese is melting and turning golden and the bases are crisp underneath. Garnish with the basil leaves and serve immediately.

Makes 2 pizzas

✳ 1 quantity Basic Pizza Dough

Topping

200 g/7 oz ready-prepared tomato pizza sauce

300 g/10½ oz canned tuna, drained

200 g/7 oz sun-dried tomatoes in oil, drained and cut into quarters, reserving 1 tbsp of the oil

50 g/1¾ oz mixed olives, stoned and halved

1 tsp dried herbes de Provence

250 g/9 oz ricotta cheese

salt and pepper

fresh basil leaves, to garnish

Chilli Tuna Pizza

1. Make the pizza dough as described on page 8. Knock back the dough by gently kneading for about a minute, then divide into two balls. To roll out the dough, flatten each ball, then, using a rolling pin, roll out on a lightly floured work surface, giving a quarter turn between each roll.

2. Preheat the oven to 220°C/425°F/Gas Mark 7. Place the pizza bases on two baking trays, using a rolling pin to transfer them from the work surface.

3. Divide the pizza sauce between the two pizza bases, spreading almost to the edges. Scatter over the tuna, tomatoes, sweetcorn, mushrooms and chilli flakes. Top with the cheese and season to taste with salt and pepper.

4. Bake in the preheated oven for 10–12 minutes, or until the cheese is melting and turning golden and the bases are crisp underneath. Serve immediately.

Makes 2 pizzas

✳ 1 quantity Basic Pizza Dough

Topping

200 g/7 oz ready-prepared tomato pizza sauce

300 g/10½ oz canned tuna, drained

6 cherry tomatoes, thinly sliced

100 g/3½ oz canned sweetcorn, drained

100 g/3½ oz button mushrooms, thinly sliced

1 tsp dried chilli flakes

250 g/9 oz mozzarella cheese in brine, drained and roughly torn

salt and pepper

Monkfish & Bacon Pizza

1. Make the pizza dough as described on page 8. Knock back the dough by gently kneading for about a minute, then divide into two balls. To roll out the dough, flatten each ball, then, using a rolling pin, roll out on a lightly floured work surface, giving a quarter turn between each roll.

2. Preheat the oven to 220°C/425°F/Gas Mark 7. Place the pizza bases on two baking trays, using a rolling pin to transfer them from the work surface.

3. Place the monkfish on a small baking tray, drizzle with the oil and season to taste with salt and pepper. Roast in the preheated oven for 18–20 minutes, or until the fish is just cooked and the flesh is opaque. Remove from the oven and flake into chunky pieces.

4. Heat a non-stick frying pan over a high heat, add the bacon and dry-fry for 2–3 minutes, or until starting to turn crispy. Remove from the pan and drain on kitchen paper.

5. Divide the pizza sauce between the two pizza bases, spreading almost to the edges. Scatter over the fish and bacon, then add the red pepper and finish with the cheese. Season to taste with salt and pepper.

6. Bake in the preheated oven for 8–10 minutes, or until the cheese is melting and golden and the bases are crisp underneath. Serve immediately.

Makes 2 pizzas

✳ 1 quantity Basic Pizza Dough

Topping
250 g/9 oz fresh monkfish fillet
1 tbsp lemon olive oil
125 g/4½ oz smoked bacon lardons
200 g/7 oz ready-prepared tomato pizza sauce
1 roasted red pepper in brine, drained and finely sliced
100 g/3½ oz mature Cheddar cheese, grated
salt and pepper

24

Smoked Salmon & Dill Pizza

1. Make the pizza dough as described on page 8. Knock back the dough by gently kneading for about a minute, then divide into two balls. To roll out the dough, flatten each ball, then, using a rolling pin, roll out on a lightly floured work surface, giving a quarter turn between each roll.

2. Preheat the oven to 230°C/450°F/Gas Mark 8. Place the pizza bases on two baking trays, using a rolling pin to transfer them from the work surface.

3. Divide the pizza sauce between the two pizza bases, spreading almost to the edges. Scatter over the salmon and spoon the ricotta in small amounts evenly over the bases. Drizzle with the dill sauce and season to taste with pepper.

4. Bake in the preheated oven for 10–12 minutes, or until the cheese is turning golden and the bases are crisp underneath. If the pizzas are browning too quickly, cover with foil for the last few minutes of cooking.

5. Garnish with the fresh rocket and serve immediately.

Makes 2 pizzas

✳ 1 quantity Basic Pizza Dough

Topping

200 g/7 oz ready-prepared tomato pizza sauce

150 g/5½ oz smoked salmon, torn into strips

250 g/9 oz ricotta cheese

2 tbsp ready-prepared dill sauce, or 2 tsp fresh dill, finely chopped

pepper

fresh rocket leaves, to garnish

25

Prawn & Mushroom Calzone

1. Make the pizza dough as described on page 8. Knock back the dough by gently kneading for about a minute, then divide into two balls. To roll out the dough, flatten each ball, then, using a rolling pin, roll out on a lightly floured work surface, giving a quarter turn between each roll.

2. Preheat the oven to 220°C/425°F/Gas Mark 7. Place the pizza bases on two baking trays, using a rolling pin to transfer them from the work surface.

3. Heat the oil in a frying pan over a medium heat. Add the garlic and mushrooms and gently sauté for 2–3 minutes. Add the prawns and cook for 1–2 minutes, until they have turned pink and are just cooked. Season to taste with salt and pepper, remove from the pan and drain on kitchen paper.

4. Spread the pizza sauce over the two pizza bases, then scatter the mushroom and prawn mixture over one half of each of the bases. Add the sweetcorn and top with the cheese.

5. Brush the edges of the bases with a little water, then fold them over the filling to make two half-moon-shaped calzones. Seal the edges by pinching them together. Make small holes in the top of each calzone with the tip of a knife.

6. Bake in the preheated oven for 10–15 minutes, or until the tops are golden and the bases are crisp underneath. Serve immediately.

Makes 2 calzones

✳ 1 quantity Basic Pizza Dough

Filling
1 tbsp olive oil

1 garlic clove, crushed

200 g/7 oz button mushrooms

200 g/7 oz raw prawns, peeled and deveined

200 g/7 oz ready-prepared tomato pizza sauce

100 g/3½ oz canned sweetcorn, drained

250 g/9 oz mozzarella cheese in brine, drained and roughly torn

salt and pepper

26

Tiger Prawn & Coriander Pesto Pizza

1. Make the pizza dough as described on page 8, adding the chilli flakes with the flour. Knock back the dough by gently kneading for about a minute, then divide into two balls. To roll out the dough, flatten each ball, then, using a rolling pin, roll out on a lightly floured work surface, giving a quarter turn between each roll.

2. Preheat the oven to 220°C/425°F/Gas Mark 7. Place the pizza bases on two baking trays, using a rolling pin to transfer them from the work surface.

3. Divide the coriander pesto between the two pizza bases, spreading almost to the edges. Scatter over the spring onions, prawns and cheese, then season to taste with salt and pepper.

4. Bake in the preheated oven for 10–12 minutes, or until the cheese is melting and turning golden and the bases are crisp underneath. Serve immediately.

Makes 2 pizzas

* 1 quantity Basic Pizza Dough

1 tsp dried chilli flakes

Topping

8 tbsp ready-prepared coriander pesto

8 spring onions, finely chopped

300 g/10½ oz cooked tiger prawns

125 g/4½ oz Parmesan cheese shavings

salt and pepper

27

Crab, Asparagus & Ricotta Cheese Pizza

1. Make the pizza dough as described on page 8. Knock back the dough by gently kneading for about a minute, then divide into four balls. To roll out the dough, flatten each ball, then, using a rolling pin, roll out on a lightly floured work surface, giving a quarter turn between each roll.

2. Preheat the oven to 220°C/425°F/Gas Mark 7. Place the pizza bases on two baking trays, using a rolling pin to transfer them from the work surface.

3. Bring a small saucepan of lightly salted water to the boil, then add the asparagus spears and cook for 2–3 minutes. Drain and plunge into ice cold water for 1–2 minutes (to retain the bright green colour). Drain well and chop roughly.

4. Divide the pizza sauce between the four pizza bases, spreading almost to the edges. Scatter over the cooked asparagus, crabmeat and onion. Top with the cheese and drizzle over the oil. Season to taste with salt and pepper.

5. Bake in the preheated oven for 10–12 minutes, or until the cheese is melting and turning golden and the bases are crisp underneath. Serve immediately.

Makes 4 small pizzas

* 1 quantity Basic Pizza Dough

Topping

150 g/5½ oz asparagus spears, trimmed

200 g/7 oz ready-prepared tomato pizza sauce

175 g/6 oz cooked white crabmeat

1 red onion, finely sliced

250 g/9 oz ricotta cheese

1 tbsp extra virgin olive oil

salt and pepper

28

Clam & Pepper Pizza

1. Make the pizza dough as described on page 8. Knock back the dough by gently kneading for about a minute, then divide into two balls. To roll out the dough, flatten each ball, then, using a rolling pin, roll out on a lightly floured work surface, giving a quarter turn between each roll.

2. Preheat the oven to 220°C/425°F/Gas Mark 7. Place the pizza bases on two baking trays, using a rolling pin to transfer them from the work surface.

3. Divide the salsa between the two pizza bases, spreading almost to the edges. Scatter over the clams, green pepper, onion and oregano and top with the mozzarella cheese and Parmesan cheese. Season to taste with salt and pepper.

4. Bake in the preheated oven for 8–10 minutes, or until the cheese is melting and turning golden and the bases are crisp underneath. Serve immediately.

Makes 2 pizzas

✳ 1 quantity Basic Pizza Dough

Topping
200 g/7 oz ready-prepared tomato salsa

280 g/10 oz canned baby clams, drained

1 green pepper, deseeded and finely sliced

1 red onion, finely sliced

1 tsp dried oregano

125 g/4½ oz mozzarella cheese in brine, drained and roughly torn

50 g/1¾ oz Parmesan cheese shavings

salt and pepper

29

Marinara Calzone

1. Make the pizza dough as described on page 8. Knock back the dough by gently kneading for about a minute, then divide into four balls. To roll out the dough, flatten each ball, then, using a rolling pin, roll out on a lightly floured work surface, giving a quarter turn between each roll. Roll each one into a circle with a diameter of about 19 cm/7½ inches.

2. Preheat the oven to 220°C/425°F/Gas Mark 7. Place the pizza bases on two baking trays, using a rolling pin to transfer them from the work surface.

3. Divide the pizza sauce between the four pizza bases, spreading almost to the edges. Scatter the seafood and basil over half of each pizza and top with the cheese. Season to taste with salt and pepper.

4. Brush the edges of the bases with a little water, then fold them over the filling to make four half-moon-shaped calzones. Seal the edges all the way around by folding a little of the dough over and pinching the edges together. Make some small holes in the top of each calzone with the tip of a knife.

5. Bake in the preheated oven for 10–15 minutes, or until the tops are golden and the bases are crisp underneath. Serve immediately.

Makes 4 small calzones

1 quantity Basic Pizza Dough

Filling

200 g/7 oz ready-prepared tomato pizza sauce

200 g/7 oz mixed cooked seafood, such as prawns, mussels and squid rings, drained well on kitchen paper

2 tbsp finely chopped fresh basil

200 g/7 oz mozzarella chese in brine, drained and roughly torn

salt and pepper

30

Seafood Pizza

1. Make the pizza dough as described on page 8, adding the rosemary with the flour. Knock back the dough by gently kneading for about a minute, then divide into two balls. To roll out the dough, flatten each ball, then, using a rolling pin, roll out on a lightly floured work surface, giving a quarter turn between each roll.

2. Preheat the oven to 220°C/425°F/Gas Mark 7. Place the pizza bases on two baking trays, using a rolling pin to transfer them from the work surface.

3. Divide the pizza sauce between the two pizza bases, spreading almost to the edges. Scatter over the seafood and onion and top with the mozzarella cheese and Parmesan cheese. Season to taste with salt and pepper.

4. Bake in the preheated oven for 10–12 minutes, or until the cheese is melting and golden and the bases are crisp underneath. Serve immediately

Makes 2 pizzas

⁎ 1 quantity Basic Pizza Dough
1 tsp dried rosemary

Topping
200 g/7 oz ready-prepared tomato pizza sauce

200 g/7 oz mixed cooked seafood, such as prawns, mussels and squid rings, drained well on kitchen paper

1 red onion, finely chopped

85 g/3 oz mozzarella cheese in brine, drained and roughly torn

85 g/3 oz Parmesan cheese shavings

salt and pepper

Nice &
Spicy

31

Triple Chilli Pizza

1. Make the pizza dough as described on page 8, adding the chilli flakes with the flour. Knock back the dough by gently kneading for about a minute then divide into two balls. To roll out the dough, flatten each ball, then, using a rolling pin, roll out on a lightly floured work surface, giving a quarter turn between each roll.

2. Preheat the grill to high, place the steak on a grill rack and cook for 10–12 minutes, turning once, or until cooked to your liking. Remove from the grill, leave to rest for 5 minutes, then slice thinly.

3. Preheat the oven to 220°C/425°F/Gas Mark 7. Place the pizza bases on two baking trays, using a rolling pin to transfer them from the work surface.

4. Spread the salsa over the pizza bases, spreading almost to the edges. Top with the steak, jalapeño peppers and red peppers. Drizzle the chipotle paste evenly over the pizzas, top with the cheese and season to taste with salt and pepper.

5. Bake in the preheated oven for 15–20 minutes, or until the cheese is melting and turning golden and the bases are crisp underneath. Serve immediately.

Makes 2 pizzas

1 quantity Basic Pizza Dough

1 tsp dried chilli flakes

Topping

350 g/12 oz rump steak, trimmed

200 g/7 oz ready-prepared tomato salsa

2 tbsp sweet, hot red jalapeño peppers in oil, drained and sliced

2 ready-roasted red peppers in brine, drained and finely sliced

1 tbsp chipotle paste

175 g/6 oz Monterey Jack cheese, grated

salt and pepper

Chilli Prawn Pizza

1. Make the pizza dough as described on page 8. Knock back the dough by gently kneading for about a minute, then divide into two balls. To roll out the dough, flatten each ball, then, using a rolling pin, roll out on a lightly floured work surface, giving a quarter turn between each roll.

2. Preheat the oven to 220°C/425°F/Gas Mark 7. Place the pizza bases on two baking trays, using a rolling pin to transfer them from the work surface.

3. Divide the pizza sauce between the two pizza bases, spreading almost to the edges. Scatter over the prawns and spring onions, drizzle over the harrissa paste and top with the cheese. Season to taste with salt and pepper.

4. Bake in the preheated oven for 10–12 minutes, or until the cheese is melting and turning golden and the bases are crisp underneath. Garnish with the fresh coriander and serve immediately.

Makes 2 pizzas

✳ 1 quantity Basic Pizza Dough

Topping

200 g/7 oz ready-prepared tomato pizza sauce

200 g/7 oz cooked, peeled prawns

½ bunch spring onions, finely chopped

1 tbsp harissa paste mixed with 1 tbsp olive oil

250 g/9 oz mozzarella cheese in brine, drained and roughly torn

salt and pepper

handful of fresh coriander, roughly chopped, to garnish

Piri Piri Chicken Pizza

1. Make the pizza dough as described on page 8. Knock back the dough by gently kneading for about a minute, then divide into two balls. To roll out the dough, flatten each ball, then, using a rolling pin, roll out on a lightly floured work surface, giving a quarter turn between each roll.

2. Place the pizza bases on two baking trays, using a rolling pin to transfer them from the work surface.

3. Place the oil in a dish and add the chicken, spices, oregano and honey. Cover and leave in the refrigerator to marinate for 1–2 hours.

4. Preheat the oven to 220°C/425°F/Gas Mark 7. Place the strips of cheese around the rim of each pizza, about 2 cm/ ¾ inch from the edges. Use a pastry brush to wet the edges, then fold over to seal the cheese inside the crust.

5. Place the marinated chicken on a baking tray and bake in the preheated oven for 15–20 minutes, or until just cooked through.

6. Divide the pizza sauce between the two pizza bases, spreading almost to the edges. Scatter over the chicken, onion, yellow pepper and cheese. Season to taste with salt and pepper.

7. Bake in the preheated oven for 12–15 minutes, or until the cheese is melting and turning golden and the bases are crisp underneath. Drizzle with the soured cream and serve immediately.

Makes 2 pizzas

* 1 quantity Basic Pizza Dough

100 g/3½ oz mozzarella cheese in brine, drained and cut into short strips

Topping
1 tbsp vegetable oil

400 g/14 oz chicken breast meat, cut into small cubes

1 tsp garlic pepper

1½ tsp paprika

1 tsp ground ginger

½ tsp cayenne pepper

1 tsp dried oregano

1 tbsp clear honey

200 g/7 oz ready-prepared tomato pizza sauce

1 red onion, finely sliced

1 yellow pepper, deseeded and finely sliced

250 g/9 oz mozzarella cheese in brine, drained and roughly torn

salt and pepper

4 tbsp soured cream, to serve

Chilli con Carne Calzone

1. Make the pizza dough as described on page 8. Knock back the dough by gently kneading for about a minute, then divide into four balls. To roll out the dough, flatten each ball, then, using a rolling pin, roll out on a lightly floured work surface to a diameter of about 19 cm/7½ inches, giving a quarter turn between each roll.

2. Preheat the oven to 220°C/425°F/Gas Mark 7. Place the pizza bases on two baking trays, using a rolling pin to transfer them from the work surface.

3. Heat the oil in a saucepan over a medium heat, add the onion and garlic and sauté for 3–4 minutes. Add the steak mince and spices and cook for 1–2 minutes. Stir in the tomato purée, canned tomatoes, water and beans and season to taste with salt and pepper. Cook for 15–20 minutes, or until the meat is cooked through and the sauce is thick.

4. Place equal amounts of the mince mixture on half of each base.

5. Brush the edges of the bases with a little water then fold them over the filling to make four half-moon-shaped calzones. Seal the edges by pinching them together. Make small holes in the top of each calzone with the tip of a knife.

6. Bake in the preheated oven for 10–15 minutes, or until the tops are golden and the bases are crisp underneath. Serve immediately.

Makes 4 small calzones

✳ 1 quantity Basic Pizza Dough

Filling
1 tbsp vegetable oil
1 onion, finely chopped
1 garlic clove, crushed
250 g/9 oz lean steak mince
1 tbsp chilli powder
1 tsp ground coriander
1 tbsp tomato purée
200 g/7 oz canned chopped tomatoes
100 ml/3½ fl oz cold water
125 g/4½ oz canned kidney beans, drained and rinsed
salt and pepper

Cajun-spiced Chicken Pizza

1. Make the pizza dough as described on page 8, adding the oregano with the flour. Knock back the dough by gently kneading for about a minute, then divide into two balls. To roll out the dough, flatten each ball, then, using a rolling pin, roll out on a lightly floured work surface, giving a quarter turn between each roll.

2. Place the pizza bases on two baking trays, using a rolling pin to transfer them from the work surface.

3. Mix half the oil with the spices, garlic and oregano. Add the chicken and stir to coat well. Cover and leave in the refrigerator to marinate for at least 1–2 hours.

4. Preheat the oven to 220°C/425°F/Gas Mark 7. Heat the remaining oil in a non-stick frying pan over a medium heat, then add the chicken and cook for 5–6 minutes, stirring regularly, until just cooked.

5. Divide the pizza sauce between the two pizza bases, spreading almost to the edges. Scatter over the chicken, onion and yellow pepper. Top with the cheese and season to taste with salt and pepper.

6. Bake in the preheated oven for 10–12 minutes, or until the cheese is melting and turning golden and the bases are crisp underneath. Serve immediately.

Makes 2 pizzas

✳ 1 quantity Basic Pizza Dough
2 tsp dried oregano

Topping

2 tbsp olive oil
1 tbsp paprika
½ tsp cayenne pepper
1 garlic clove, crushed
2 tsp dried oregano
400 g/14 oz chicken breast meat, cut into small strips
200 g/7 oz ready-prepared tomato pizza sauce
1 red onion, finely sliced
1 yellow pepper, deseeded and finely sliced
250 g/9 oz mozzarella cheese in brine, drained and roughly torn
salt and pepper

Pizza Mexicana

1. Make the pizza dough as described on page 8. Knock back the dough by gently kneading for about a minute. Using a rolling pin, roll out the dough to a 38 x 26-cm/15 x 10½-inch rectangle on a lightly floured work surface.

2. Heat the oil in a medium-sized saucepan over a medium heat. Add the onion and garlic and gently sauté for 3–4 minutes, until starting to soften. Add the chillies and red pepper and cook for a further 1–2 minutes, then add the steak mince and cook over a medium-high heat for 4-5 minutes, until lightly browned all over.

3. Add the tomato purée and cook for 1 minute, stirring constantly. Stir in the water and beans and season to taste with salt and pepper. Cover and simmer for 15–20 minutes, stirring occasionally, until the meat is thoroughly cooked and the sauce is spreadable. Remove from the heat and leave to cool.

4. Preheat the oven to 220°C/425°F/Gas Mark 7. Place the pizza base on a 38 x 26-cm/15 x 10½-inch rectangular baking tray, using a rolling pin to transfer it from the work surface.

5. Spread the salsa over the pizza base, then top with the beef mixture. Scatter over the jalapeño peppers and cheese and bake in the oven for 15–20 minutes, or until the cheese is melting and turning golden and the base is crisp underneath. Garnish with the guacamole and fresh coriander and serve immediately.

Makes 1 large pizza

✳ 1 quantity Basic Pizza Dough

Topping

1 tbsp vegetable oil

1 onion, finely chopped

2 garlic cloves, crushed

2 red chillies, deseeded and finely chopped

1 red pepper, deseeded and chopped

400 g/14 oz lean steak mince

2 tbsp tomato purée

100 ml/3½ fl oz cold water

250 g/9 oz canned black beans, drained and rinsed

200 g/7 oz ready-prepared spicy salsa

50 g/1¾ oz sweet, hot red jalapeño peppers in oil, drained and sliced

200 g/7 oz Cheddar cheese, grated

salt and pepper

4 tbsp ready-prepared guacamole and fresh chopped coriander, to garnish

Pork Meatball Pizza

1. Make the pizza dough as described on page 8. Knock back the dough by gently kneading for about a minute. Using a rolling pin, roll out the dough to a 38 x 26-cm/15 x 10½-inch rectangle on a lightly floured work surface.

2. Heat 1 tablespoon of the oil in a frying pan over a medium heat. Add the onion and garlic and fry for 3–4 minutes. Leave to cool slightly, then mix with the pork mince, sage and chilli. Season to taste with salt and pepper.

3. Form the mixture into small balls about the size of walnuts. Heat the remaining oil in a frying pan over a medium–high heat, add the meatballs and fry for about 10 minutes, turning regularly until cooked through.

4. Preheat the oven to 220°C/425°F/Gas Mark 7. Place the pizza base on a 38 x 26-cm/15 x 10½-inch rectangular baking tray, using a rolling pin to transfer it from the work surface.

5. Spread the pizza sauce over the base almost to the edges, top with the meatballs, green pepper and cheese and season to taste with salt and pepper.

6. Bake in the preheated oven for 15–20 minutes, or until the cheese is melting and turning golden and the base is crisp underneath. Serve immediately.

Makes 1 large pizza

✳ 1 quantity Basic Pizza Dough

Topping
3 tbsp vegetable oil
1 onion, finely grated
2 garlic cloves, crushed
500 g/1lb 2 oz pork mince
1 tbsp dried sage
1 red chilli, deseeded and finely chopped
200 g/7 oz ready-prepared tomato pizza sauce
1 green pepper, deseeded and finely chopped
200 g/7 oz Cheddar cheese, grated
salt and pepper

Chorizo, Artichoke & Olive Pizza

1. Make the pizza dough as described on page 8. Knock back the dough by gently kneading for about a minute, then divide into two balls. To roll out the dough, flatten each ball, then, using a rolling pin, roll out on a lightly floured work surface, giving a quarter turn between each roll.

2. Preheat the oven to 220°C/425°F/Gas Mark 7. Place the pizza bases on two baking trays, using a rolling pin to transfer them from the work surface.

3. Divide the pizza sauce between the two pizza bases, spreading almost to the edges. Scatter over the chorizo, artichoke hearts and olives and top with the Manchego cheese and mozzarella cheese. Season to taste with pepper.

4. Bake in the preheated oven for 10–12 minutes, or until the cheese is melting and turning golden and the bases are crisp underneath. Cover with foil for the last few minutes of cooking if the chorizo starts to brown too quickly. Serve immediately.

Makes 2 pizzas

✳ 1 quantity Basic Pizza Dough

Topping

200 g/7 oz ready-prepared tomato pizza sauce

175 g/6 oz spicy chorizo, thinly sliced

150 g/5½ oz artichoke hearts in vegetable oil, drained and sliced into quarters

50 g/1¾ oz Spanish anchovy- or chilli-stuffed olives in garlic oil, drained and halved

100 g/3½ oz Manchego cheese, grated

100 g/3½ oz mozzarella cheese in brine, drained and roughly torn

pepper

39

Chilli-crust Pepperoni Pizza

1. Make the pizza dough as described on page 8, adding the chilli flakes with the flour. Knock back the dough by gently kneading for about a minute, then divide into two balls. To roll out the dough, flatten each ball, then, using a rolling pin, roll out on a lightly floured work surface, giving a quarter turn between each roll.

2. Preheat the oven to 220°C/425°F/Gas Mark 7. Place the pizza bases on two baking trays, using a rolling pin to transfer them from the work surface.

3. Divide the pizza sauce between the two pizza bases, spreading almost to the edges. Top with the onion, pepperoni, mushrooms and yellow pepper. Scatter over the cheese and season to taste with pepper.

4. Bake in the preheated oven for 10–12 minutes, or until the cheese is melting and golden and the bases are crisp underneath. Serve immediately.

Makes 2 pizzas

* 1 quantity Basic Pizza Dough
1 tsp dried chilli flakes

Topping
200 g/7 oz ready-prepared tomato pizza sauce
1 red onion, finely sliced
200 g/7 oz hot pepperoni sausage, thinly sliced
100 g/3½ oz button mushrooms, thinly sliced
1 yellow pepper, deseeded and thinly sliced
200 g/7 oz Monterey Jack cheese, grated
pepper

40

Spicy Pepper &
Goat's Cheese Pizza

1. Make the pizza dough as described on page 8. Knock back the dough by gently kneading for about a minute, then divide into two balls. To roll out the dough, flatten each ball, then, using a rolling pin, roll out on a lightly floured work surface, giving a quarter turn between each roll.

2. Preheat the oven to 200°C/400°F/Gas Mark 6. Place the pizza bases on two baking trays, using a rolling pin to transfer them from the work surface.

3. Place the onion, red pepper, yellow pepper, chillies and garlic on a baking tray, drizzle over the oil, season to taste with salt and pepper and toss well to coat. Place in the preheated oven and cook for 20–25 minutes, or until softened and starting to char around the edges.

4. Divide the pizza sauce between the two pizza bases, spreading almost to the edges. Scatter over the roasted vegetables and top with the cheese.

5. Bake in the preheated oven for 10–12 minutes, or until the cheese is melting and turning golden and the bases are crisp underneath. Serve immediately.

Makes 2 pizzas

✳ 1 quantity Basic Pizza Dough

Topping
1 onion, thinly sliced

1 red pepper, deseeded and finely sliced

1 yellow pepper, deseeded and finely sliced

2 red chillies, deseeded and roughly chopped

2 garlic cloves, crushed

1 tbsp extra virgin olive oil

175 g/6 oz ready-prepared tomato pizza sauce

200 g/7 oz soft goat's cheese, thinly sliced

salt and pepper

Novelty

41

Valentine's Pizza

1. Make the pizza dough as described on page 8. Knock back the dough by gently kneading for about a minute, then divide into two balls. To roll out the dough, flatten each ball, then, using a rolling pin, roll out on a lightly floured work surface, giving a quarter turn between each roll. Using your hands, shape each piece of dough into a heart shape.

2. Preheat the oven to 200°C/400°F/Gas Mark 6. Place the pizza bases on two baking trays, using a rolling pin to transfer them from the work surface.

3. Heat the vegetable oil in a frying pan over a medium–high heat. Add the scallops and bacon and sauté for 3–4 minutes. Remove from the pan and drain on kitchen paper.

4. Divide the pizza sauce between the two bases, spreading almost to the edges. Arrange the scallops and bacon evenly over the pizzas. Top with the cheese and season to taste with pepper.

5. Bake in the preheated oven for 10–15 minutes, or until the cheese is melting and turning golden and the bases are crisp underneath. Pile the rocket onto the pizzas, add a drizzle of olive oil and serve immediately.

Makes 2 pizzas

✳ 1 quantity Basic Pizza Dough

Topping

1 tsp vegetable oil

100 g/3½ oz roeless scallops, halved horizontally

100 g/3½ oz smoked bacon, chopped

200 g/7 oz ready-prepared tomato pizza sauce

200 g/7 oz Camembert cheese, sliced

pepper

fresh rocket leaves and extra virgin olive oil, to serve

42

Mini Pizza Canapés

1. Make the pizza dough as described on page 8. Knock back the dough by gently kneading for about a minute. Divide the dough into 24 balls and, using a rolling pin, roll them into small, flat circles on a lightly floured work surface.

2. Preheat the oven to 190°C/ 375°F/Gas Mark 5. Place the dough circles on several baking trays. Lay a sheet of baking paper over each tray of pizza bases and cover with a light baking tray to prevent the dough rising during cooking.

3. Bake in the preheated oven for 8–10 minutes, then remove the baking tray and paper and return to the oven for a further 5 minutes, or until they are light brown in colour. Remove from the oven and leave to cool.

4. Spoon a little soured cream onto each pizza base, then top with a piece of smoked salmon and season to taste with pepper. Garnish with the fresh chives and serve.

Makes 24 mini pizzas

✳ 1 quantity Basic Pizza Dough

Topping

100 ml/3½ fl oz soured cream

100 g/3½ oz smoked salmon pieces, rolled

pepper

finely snipped fresh chives, to garnish

43

Shaped Pizzas

1. Make the pizza dough as described on page 8. Knock back the dough by gently kneading for about a minute, then divide into two balls. Using a rolling pin, roll out each ball on a lightly floured work surface. Form the dough into shapes of your choice, either by hand or with large, fun-shaped cookie cutters.

2. Preheat the oven to 220°C/425°F/ Gas Mark 7. Place the pizza bases on two baking trays, using a rolling pin to transfer them from the work surface.

3. Divide the barbecue sauce between the bases, spreading almost to the edges. Scatter over the chicken and sweetcorn and top with the cheese.

4. Place in the preheated oven for 10–12 minutes (slightly less for mini pizzas), or until the cheese is melting and turning golden and the bases are crisp underneath. Serve immediately.

Makes 2 regular pizzas or several smaller pizzas

✳ 1 quantity Basic Pizza Dough

Topping
200 g/7 oz ready-prepared barbecue sauce

100 g/3½ oz cooked chicken, sliced

100 g/3½ oz canned sweetcorn, drained

85 g/3 oz mild Cheddar cheese, grated

44

All Day Breakfast Calzone

1. Make the pizza dough as described on page 8. Knock back the dough by gently kneading for about a minute, then divide into two balls. To roll out the dough, flatten each ball, then, using a rolling pin, roll out on a lightly floured work surface, giving a quarter turn between each roll.

2. Preheat the oven to 200°C/400°F/Gas Mark 6. Place the pizza bases on two baking trays, using a rolling pin to transfer them from the work surface.

3. Drain the baked beans into a bowl, adding two to three tablespoons of the reserved liquid. Add the bacon, mushrooms and Worcestershire sauce and season to taste with salt and pepper.

4. Spread the mixture onto one half of each of the bases. Brush the edges of the bases with a little water, then fold them over the filling to make two half-moon-shaped calzones. Seal the edges by folding a little of the dough over and pinching the edges together. Make small holes in the top of each calzone with the tip of a knife.

5. Bake in the preheated oven for 10–15 minutes, or until the tops are golden and the bases are crisp underneath. Serve immediately.

Makes 2 calzones

❋ 1 quantity Basic Pizza Dough

Filling

225 g/8 oz canned baked beans

100 g/3½ oz bacon rashers, cooked and chopped

100 g/3½ oz mushrooms, thinly sliced

dash of Worcestershire sauce

salt and pepper

45

St Patrick's Day Pizza

1. Make the pizza dough as described on page 8. Knock back the dough by gently kneading for about a minute, then divide into two balls. To roll out the dough, flatten each ball, then, using a rolling pin, roll out on a lightly floured work surface, giving a quarter turn between each roll.

2. Preheat the oven to 200°C/400°F/Gas Mark 6. Place the pizza bases on two baking trays, using a rolling pin to transfer them from the work surface.

3. Divide the pizza sauce between the two pizza bases, spreading almost to the edges. Scatter over the leek, corned beef and sweetcorn and top with the cheese. Season to taste with salt and pepper.

4. Bake in the preheated oven for 10–12 minutes, or until the cheese is melting and turning golden and the bases are crisp underneath. Serve immediately.

Makes 2 pizzas

* 1 quantity Basic Pizza Dough

Topping
200 g/7 oz ready-prepared tomato pizza sauce

1 leek, finely chopped

150 g/5½ oz corned beef, chopped

150 g/5½ oz canned sweetcorn, drained

150 g/5½ oz Cheddar cheese, grated

salt and pepper

46

Halloween Special Pizza

1. Make the pizza dough as described on page 8. Knock back the dough by gently kneading for about a minute, then divide into two balls. To roll out the dough, flatten each ball, then, using a rolling pin, roll out on a lightly floured work surface, giving a quarter turn between each roll.

2. Preheat the oven to 220°C/425°F/Gas Mark 7. Place the pizza bases on two baking trays, using a rolling pin to transfer them from the work surface.

3. Place the pumpkin on a baking tray, drizzle over the oil and add the thyme. Season to taste with salt and pepper and toss well to coat. Place in the preheated oven and roast for 15 minutes, or until softened and starting to char around the edges.

4. Divide the pizza sauce between the two pizza bases, spreading almost to the edges. Scatter over the pumpkin and the onion, then top with the cheese and season to taste with salt and pepper.

5. Return to the oven and bake for 10–12 minutes, or until the cheese is melting and turning golden and the bases are crisp underneath. Serve immediately.

Makes 2 pizzas

✳ 1 quantity Basic Pizza Dough

Topping
400 g/14 oz pumpkin or butternut squash, peeled, deseeded and cut into small cubes

1 tbsp extra virgin olive oil

1 tsp dried thyme

200 g/7 oz ready-prepared tomato pizza sauce

1 red onion, finely sliced

125 g/4½ oz Gruyère cheese, grated

salt and pepper

47

Apple Pie Pizza

1. Make the pizza dough as described on page 8, adding the cinnamon with the flour. Knock back the dough by gently kneading for about a minute, then divide into two balls. To roll out the dough, flatten each ball, then, using a rolling pin, roll out on a lightly floured work surface, giving a quarter turn between each roll.

2. Preheat the oven to 230°C/450°F/Gas Mark 8. Place the pizza bases on two baking trays, using a rolling pin to transfer them from the work surface.

3. Melt the butter in a heavy-based non-stick frying pan over a medium heat. Add the sugar, stirring well to dissolve. Leave to bubble for 5–6 minutes, until dark and syrupy. Add the apples, raisins and cloves and cook for a further 4–5 minutes, until the apples are starting to soften but are not completely cooked.

4. Using a slotted spoon divide the apple and raisin mixture between the two pizza bases. Spoon over about half the syrup, reserving the remainder.

5. Bake in the preheated oven for 8–10 minutes, or until the bases are crisp underneath. Drizzle over the reserved syrup, dust with icing sugar and serve warm.

Makes 2 pizzas

* 1 quantity Basic Pizza Dough
1 tsp ground cinnamon

Topping
3 tbsp butter

100 g/3½ oz soft light brown sugar

3 large eating apples, peeled, cored and thickly sliced

50 g/1¾ oz raisins

pinch of ground cloves

icing sugar, for dusting

48

S'mores Special Pizza

1. Make the pizza dough as described on page 8. Knock back the dough by gently kneading for about a minute, then divide into two balls. To roll out the dough, flatten each ball, then, using a rolling pin, roll out on a lightly floured work surface, giving a quarter turn between each roll.

2. Preheat the oven to 220°C/425°F/Gas Mark 7. Place the pizza bases on two baking trays, using a rolling pin to transfer them from the work surface.

3. Divide the chocolate spread between the two pizza bases, spreading almost to the edges. Top with the cookies, marshmallows and chocolate chunks.

4. Bake in the preheated oven for 8–10 minutes, or until the bases are crisp underneath. Cover with foil for the last few minutes of cooking if the tops start to brown too much. Dust with icing sugar and serve warm with the mascarpone cheese, if using.

Makes 2 pizzas

✴ 1 quantity Basic Pizza Dough

Topping

6 tbsp chocolate spread

100 g/3½ oz chocolate chip cookies, roughly chopped

50 g/1¾ oz mini marshmallows

85 g/3 oz milk chocolate, broken into chunks

icing sugar, for dusting

175 g/6 oz mascarpone cheese, to serve (optional)

49

Festive Pizza

1. Make the pizza dough as described on page 8. Knock back the dough by gently kneading for about a minute, then divide into two balls. To roll out the dough, flatten each ball, then, using a rolling pin, roll out on a lightly floured work surface, giving a quarter turn between each roll.

2. Preheat the oven to 220°C/425°F/Gas Mark 7. Place the pizza bases on two baking trays, using a rolling pin to transfer them from the work surface.

3. Divide the pizza sauce between the two pizza bases, spreading almost to the edges. Mix the stuffing with the redcurrant sauce and crumble over the pizza bases. Top with the turkey and cheese and season to taste with salt and pepper.

4. Bake in the preheated oven for 10–12 minutes, or until the cheese is melting and turning golden and the bases are crisp underneath. Garnish with the chopped parsley and serve immediately.

Makes 2 pizzas

* 1 quantity Basic Pizza Dough

Topping
200 g/7 oz ready-prepared tomato pizza sauce

100 g/3½ oz ready-prepared stuffing mixture

4 tbsp redcurrant sauce

150 g/5½ oz shredded cooked turkey

200 g/7oz Gruyère cheese, grated

salt and pepper

chopped fresh flat-leaf parsley, to garnish

50

Cherry Pie &
Mascarpone Pizza

1. Make the pizza dough as described on page 8. Knock back the dough by gently kneading for about a minute, then divide into two balls. To roll out the dough, flatten each ball, then, using a rolling pin, roll out on a lightly floured work surface, giving a quarter turn between each roll.

2. Preheat the oven to 220°C/425°F/Gas Mark 7. Place the pizza bases on two baking trays, using a rolling pin to transfer them from the work surface.

3. Cover each base with a piece of baking paper and a light baking tray to prevent the dough rising during cooking. Bake in the preheated oven for 8–10 minutes, then remove the baking tray and paper and return to the oven for a further 3–5 minutes, or until lightly browned.

4. Spread the mascarpone cheese evenly over the pizza bases and spoon over the cherry pie filling. Dust generously with icing sugar and serve immediately.

Makes 2 pizzas

* 1 quantity Basic Pizza Dough

Topping

200 g/7 oz mascarpone cheese

200 g/7 oz canned cherry pie filling, warmed

icing sugar, for dusting